Jewelry Making 1-2-3
45+ Simple Projects

Karin Van Voorhees

KALMBACH BOOKS

Jewelry Making 1-2-3
45+ Simple Projects

Karin Van Voorhees

WAUKESHA, WI

Kalmbach Books
21027 Crossroads Circle
Waukesha, Wisconsin 53186
www.JewelryAndBeadingStore.com

Published in 2015
19 18 17 16 15   1 2 3 4 5

Manufactured in China

ISBN: 978-1-62700-180-9
EISBN: 978-1-62700-181-6

Editor: Erica Swanson
Book Design: Lisa Bergman
Photographers: James Forbes, William Zuback

Library of Congress Control Number: 2014958385

Contents

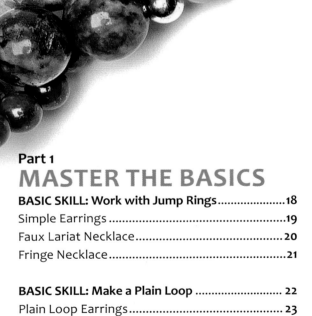

Introduction

Stringing beads…it's a skill most of us mastered in nursery school with some painted pasta and twine. See? You've already got what it takes to make all the jewelry in this book!

I've been making jewelry in one form or another (macaroni beads and beach finds included) for most of my life, and I've been making it professionally for more than 10 years. What I've discovered is that it really comes down to three basic ideas: Master the basics, keep it simple, and let the materials tell the story.

I put this collection of easy-to-create jewelry together for you, so you can string a handful of beads on a wire or headpin and walk out the door a few hours later wearing a fabulous necklace or pair of earrings. I'll teach you what you need to know and help you with some of the common obstacles. Using basic techniques and applying simple design ideas will make your jewelry long-lasting and beautiful.

One of the things I love about stringing jewelry is that no two pieces need to be the same. This book has a wide range of colors and styles and I'm confident you'll find many projects to make that suit your taste. I shopped for the materials for this book everywhere—

national and regional bead shows, local bead stores, craft chains, and discount retailers. I've got some fabulous plastic beads and base-metal clasps as well as pricier gemstones and sterling silver findings. You'll see that the design and execution are probably more important than the materials, and there's no "right" or "wrong"—just choose what you love and take it from there.

> "This book has a wide range of colors and styles and I'm confident you'll find many projects to make that suit your taste."

Look for an explanation of the many kinds of beads on page 10.

In addition to beads, you'll need findings—all the bits and pieces that hold the jewelry together—such as headpins and earring wires. Find detailed descriptions of these on page 12. Luckily for jewelry makers, style and material choices have exploded in recent years. You should have no trouble sourcing what you need at your local bead shop or craft store.

In any endeavor, proper tools make the job easier. You'll only need four tools for the projects in this book: two pairs of pliers, wire cutters, and crimpers. Learn more about tools in the tools overview on page 14.

Once you've brushed up on the materials and tools required, you'll be ready to start making projects. Here's how this book is organized:

The first chapter of *Jewelry Making 1-2-3* explores basic techniques. Each technique or skill is taught with simple step-by-step instructions and photographs. Then, it's followed by three practice projects. The first one is super simple, the second one adds a little more detail, and the third version might take you a little longer, but is just as easy as the first.

The second and third parts of this book take a closer look at jewelry design. It's so tempting to use lots of different beads in a pattern and to add extra dangles and doo-dads thinking you're making your jewelry look more professional, when actually you're only a few beads away from a hot mess. I want you to slow down and choose carefully. Style icon Coco Chanel said *"Before leaving the house, a lady should stop, look in the mirror, and remove one piece of jewelry."* Keep this in mind as you gather your beads for a project. Less is usually more. Projects in these chapters will help you learn to make choices as you approach your jewelry making projects.

Chapter 2 takes a closer look at simple design ideas, and helps you make choices that will create stunning jewelry without going overboard.

Chapter 3 focuses on materials, such as focal pendants, earthy neutrals, or bold brights. The goal of this chapter is to help you maximize the impact of the materials you choose to create jewelry with. At the end of this chapter, I experiment with changing one element, such as a clasp, and keeping the rest of the design the same. By looking at this jewelry side by side, I hope you'll be able to see the impact that small design choices have on the final piece.

The book concludes with a Techniques Review, giving you a handy reference for all the skills learned in the book.

"You can make beautiful jewelry. Are you ready?

Let's do this!"

Materials and Tools

Every hobby has its own jargon and terminology. This section is designed to give you an overview of the materials and tools common in jewelry making. I've limited it to only the items used in this book.

Beads

Seed beads are tiny glass beads that seem to come in an endless array of colors and finishes. They can be woven into intricately patterned fabrics and stitched into complex jewelry. For stringing purposes, they make excellent spacers and are an easy way to add a splash of color to your design. They range in size from tiny size 15° beads to much larger size 6° beads; 11° is a popular size. You can purchase them in tubes, on temporary strands displayed in bunches called hanks, or in pre-mixed assortments. I love the mixes for stringing and you'll see that I use them often in this book.

Crystals add sparkle and flash to your beading designs. The best quality crystals are made in Austria by Swarovski. There are hundreds of shapes and colors to choose from.

The Czech Republic is known for its glass and crystal beads, available in many shapes and sizes. **Czech beads** can be round, rondelle (a squashed round), or formed into shapes like flowers and leaves. Czech crystals are an economic alternative and give a warm, rich look to jewelry designs.

Lampwork beads are formed by layering molten glass around rods (mandrels). Beads are finished in a kiln.

Polymer clay beads are like miniature works of art. Made from modeling clay and baked to finish, these small treasures can be elaborate or whimsical. Polymer clay beads bring color and pattern to your work.

Gemstone beads are formed from natural rocks such as quartz, garnet, amazonite, turquoise, and many more. Shapes include nuggets, rounds, ovals, rectangles, briolettes, and rondelles, and finishes can be smooth, faceted, or natural. Most gemstones have been stabilized, some have been dyed to enhance or change the color, and some are laboratory manufactured. Gemstone beads should be marked "natural" or "synthetic." Grades, from A to D, reveal the quality of the stone. Look carefully as you select. You may find a lower grade still meets your standards and will cost you much less. Gemstones are usually sold on 15- or 16-in. (38–41cm) strands in bead stores, and shorter strands in craft stores.

For centuries, people have been making beads and adornments from natural materials including **wood**, **bones**, **nuts**, **shells**, and **seeds**, and the tradition continues today. I've used a few of these natural beads in these jewelry projects.

Cultured **freshwater pearls** provide organic beauty and deep luster. Many have been dyed to achieve a broad range of colors. (Soak pearls in water to help remove excess dye before you string them.) Shapes include round, rice, rondelle, potato, keishi, stick, and coin. Pearls usually have small holes, but larger-hole varieties are available for use with leather and cord.

Gold-filled, sterling silver, plated, and base **metal beads** can be found in many sizes, textures, and shapes. Spacer beads help accent a focal bead or extend a pattern. Decorative beads give substance to your jewelry. Silver beads can be imported from Thailand, Bali, India, and other countries.

Manufactured beads from **Lucite**, **plastic**, and **resin** are both new and vintage. Lucite is a trademark for acrylic resin; vintage Lucite beads can be highly collectible. Plastic beads are an inexpensive way to get started in this hobby. Because they are lightweight, jewelry made with plastic beads can be comfortable to wear. Resin beads have been cast and molded.

Findings

The term "finding" refers to all the odds and ends that come together to turn your beads into a piece of finished jewelry. These include:

Sterling silver and gold-filled **wire** is most common, but there are other choices available, including base metal wire such as copper and other craft wires. When purchasing wire, first consider gauge. Gauge is determined by the diameter of the wire (its thickness), and the larger the number, the thinner the wire. 22-gauge is a good working wire. 26-gauge is thin enough to go through small holes, such as those in pearls. 18-gauge is thick and is better for sturdier projects. Wire is also marked by hardness. Half-hard wire is comfortable to work with and will suit any project in this book.

Headpins are short lengths of wire. They hold beads in place and can be used for embellishments and connections. Plain headpins resemble a nail, and decorative headpins have a fancy end; you'll find them in 1–3-in. (2.5–7.6cm) lengths and several gauges of wire.

Chain comes in lots of shapes, sizes, and textures. Choose sterling silver or gold filled, or base metal chain such as copper or gunmetal. Cable and curb chain are common; other choices include long-and-short, rolo, twisted curb, and many decorative links.

Flexible beading wire is the foundation of all strung jewelry. It's very different than the metal wire described above—it appears to be as thin as thread. It's made of bundles of steel wire bound together and coated with clear nylon. The diameter is how thin or thick the wire is: .012 is very thin, .014 is average, and .019 is thicker. The strength and flexibility depends on the number of wire bundles inside, usually in multiples of seven. The more wire bundles, the more flexible and strong the beading wire is. Flexible beading wire is available in many colors, as well as in silver and gold plating. For the projects in this book, I

used .014 wire. When the wire was exposed as part of the design, I used SoftFlex 925 Sterling Silver Extreme Flex wire.

Elastic can be a single or monofilament strand such as Stretch Magic, or a flat ribbon-like strand made of many filaments bonded together, such as Gossamer Floss. I prefer ribbon elastic for beading. Use a beading needle to string the beads; the flat cord will hold a knot well.

Jump rings are connectors. Choose well-made, sturdy jump rings that will hold their shape. Thicker gauges work when the jump rings are part of the design. Jump rings are sold "open" or soldered and are round or oval in shape. Split rings are like tiny key chains. The spiral of wire keeps whatever you've attached—a link of chain, a dangle with a loop, or a manufactured charm—in place.

Earring wires turn your dangle into an earring. They are available in many styles. Hook-shaped and lever-back are popular, as are hoop-style, post-back, and screw-backs. Many of the hook-shaped styles have extra embellishments, including beads, springs, charms, or gemstones. Ear nuts or clutches anchor the back of an earring post or wire. Changing earring wire styles can make a big difference in your final look.

Crimp tubes are the finishing security for any strung project. I prefer sterling silver 1x2mm crimp tubes. They flatten into a nice square or they fold easily for a slim profile. They are strong and provide a secure finish. Base metal crimp beads or tubes can be weaker; I often use two instead of one just to be safe. Crimp covers are little clamshell-shaped beads that fold over a crimp bead and look like a round bead. They are especially useful in designs where the crimp is in a visible place.

Fold-over crimps, **crimp ends**, **pinch ends**, and **end crimps** are used to finish cord, ribbon, and other fibers. Many styles and finishes are available. Match the size to the diameter of your cord.

Clasps are as important to your design as any other element. You want a functional clasp but you also want to consider one that balances the weight of your piece, complements your design, is pretty to look at, and easy to use. Toggle clasps, also called bar-and-loop clasps, work with the tension of the bracelet or necklace to stay closed. Sometimes it's hard to maneuver the bar end—simply string a few extra round spacer beads on that side, and you'll be pleased with the added flexibility. Spring clasps are round "trigger" clasps and hook to a jump ring or a link of chain. Lobster claw clasps are similar to spring clasps in construction, but the shape resembles a lobster's claw. S-clasps and hook clasps hook into a large ring. Box clasps are elegant, and often have several loops so they are ideal for multistrand jewelry. Slide clasps also provide a secure, attractive connection for multistrand pieces. Part 3 gives you some options for choosing clasps to suit your design.

Beadcaps are cup-shaped half circles with holes that cradle a bead and provide an ornate, sophisticated look. Part 2 explores integrating beadcaps into your jewelry design.

Cones are usually metal, and are tapered. They are primarily used to draw multiple beaded strands into one smooth finish. Used creatively, cones can top tassels, or make an attractive finish to beaded dangle earrings.

13

Tools

You'll only need four tools for the projects in this book. You can purchase tools at bead stores, craft stores, or online from manufacturers. There are wide ranges in quality. I started out with inexpensive tools and they've served me well. I've never needed to upgrade, although I've been tempted many times. Consider comfort and ergonomics. As with most repetitive tasks, jewelry making can take a toll on your hands!

Roundnose pliers have round, tapered jaws and are used most often to form loops. Control the size of the loops by the position of the wire on the shaft of the pliers.

Chainnose pliers have a smooth, flat, tapered jaw. They are great for getting into small spaces, such as finishing a wrapped loop. Use chainnose pliers to flatten a crimp bead. They also are ideal for opening and closing jump rings, as the smooth jaw provides a tight grasp on the metal. Start with one pair, but if you are doing a lot of work with jump rings you may want a second pair.

Crimping pliers produce a folded crimp in a two-step process. Folded crimps are a professional-looking finish for any strung jewelry; they also are smaller, so they can be hidden in a crimp cover or large-hole bead.

Diagonal wire cutters cut headpins, wire, and beading wire with a nice, diagonal edge which is perfect for finishing wrapped loops. Most diagonal wire cutters have a back edge that cuts flush, which is desirable for trimming wire ends.

In addition to these core hand tools, you'll also need a few extras for your workspace:

Use a **ruler** to measure your beaded work. Use a **flexible measuring tape** to measure around wrists and necks to determine your finished length.

Flexible beading needles have a large eye that's easy to thread, but it completely collapses as it's drawn through the bead, so you can string pearls or other small-hole beads with ease. Beading needles are most often used with ribbon elastic.

Bead stoppers are very helpful. This little lifesaver keeps the beads from spilling off the end of a wire during a stringing project, without leaving a sticky residue like tape does. Each clamp can hold several wires, so it works for multistrand projects as well.

Most often, I use **G-S Hypo Cement**, a strong, jewelry-grade glue that provides a flexible bond. That's important, because when you wear your jewelry it will move with you. A rigid glue could flake or chip off over time. I also like the needle-nose applicator which helps me get the right amount of glue into the right spot. Occasionally, I use **superglue** before adding a crimp end. One project in this book calls for superglue.

Master the Basics

1

Haste makes waste and without round loops, secure crimps, and a perfect fit, your jewelry won't hold up to multiple wearings. Take time to learn the skills first so your ends won't poke or snag, your beads won't spill, and your necklace or bracelet will have a custom fit.

BASIC SKILL

Work with jump rings

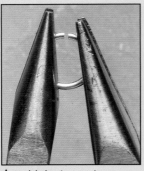

▲ Hold the jump ring with two pairs of chain-nose pliers, as shown.

▲ Open the ring by bringing one pair of pliers toward you and pushing the other pair away from you.

▲ String materials on the open ring as desired. To close, reverse the steps.

tip Never pull the ring sides out to open a jump ring. Once the metal loses its perfect curve, it will never meet properly again.

Simple earrings

1. Open a jump ring.
2. String a bead and an earring wire.
3. Close the jump ring.

Materials

2 10mm 16-gauge jump rings

2 large-hole beads

Pair of earring wires

2 5mm jump rings, optional

To change the dangle's orientation, connect the large beaded jump ring and the earring wire with a smaller jump ring, as in the top pair.

Faux lariat necklace

Materials

Finished length: 26 in. (66cm) with 3-in. (7.6cm) dangle

31 in. (79cm) cable chain cut into a 26-in. (66cm), a 3-in. (7.6cm), and a 2-in. (5cm) piece

3 12mm jump rings

2 large-hole beads

This necklace is designed to slip over your head. If you'd like a shorter necklace, follow the directions in steps 3 and 4 of the next project to connect the dangle to the center link, and attach a clasp to one end of the chain.

1. Open a 12mm jump ring. String a 3-in. (7.6cm) chain, a 2-in. (5cm) chain, and each end of a 26-in. (66cm) chain. Close the jump ring.
2. Open a 12mm jump ring. String a large-hole bead and the end of the 3-in. chain. Close the jump ring.
3. Repeat step 2 with the end of the 2-in. chain.

Fringe necklace

Materials

Finished length: 17 in. (43cm)
with 2-in. (5cm) dangle

1 yd. (.9m) cable chain cut
into **1** 16-in. (41cm) and
10 2-in. (5cm) pieces

12mm jump ring

13 7mm jump rings

10 6° seed beads

Lobster claw clasp

 tip Find the center link
of chain by stringing
each end link on a
headpin. Watch the
drape of the necklace,
and the center link
will drop down
from the rest.

1. Open a 7mm jump ring. String a 6° seed bead
and one end of a 2-in. (5cm) chain. Close the
jump ring. Repeat with all of the 2-in. chains.

2. Open the 12mm jump ring, and string the
unadorned end of each 2-in. chain. Close the
jump ring.

3. Find the center link of the 16-in. (41cm) chain.
Open a 7mm jump ring and connect the dangle
from step 2 and the center link of chain. Close
the jump ring.

4. Use a 7mm jump ring to attach a lobster claw
clasp to one end of the 16-in. chain. Attach a
7mm jump ring to the other end.

Make a plain loop

▲ To make a plain loop above a bead, trim the end of the wire or headpin to ⅜ in. (1cm), and bend it at a right angle against the bead. (To make a plain loop at the end of a wire, grasp the wire with chainnose pliers ⅜ in. from the end and make a right-angle bend.)

▲ Grasp the tip of the wire with roundnose pliers, and feel to be sure that the wire is flush with the edge of the pliers. If you feel a stub of wire, you've grasped too far away from the tip, so adjust your pliers. Gently roll the wire until you can't roll comfortably anymore.

▲ Reposition the pliers, and continue to roll the loop. The tip of the wire should meet the corner of your initial bend, and you should have a perfect, centered wire circle.

OPEN AND CLOSE A PLAIN LOOP

▲ To open a formed loop, grasp it with two pairs of pliers, held parallel to each other. Gently push the loop open by moving one pair of pliers forward and the other pair backward.

▲ Repeat the process in reverse to close the loop. Resist the temptation to "unroll" the loop—this will overwork the wire and weaken it, and you'll never get a perfectly round loop the second time.

Plain loop earrings

Materials

2 20–25mm links or large jump rings

2 10x6mm rondelle-shaped beads (these are Czech glass with a Picasso finish)

2 decorative headpins

Pair of earring wires

1. Create a dangle: String a bead on a headpin and make a plain loop.
2. Open an earring wire, and connect the dangle and a link. Close the earring wire.
3. Make a second earring.

another option

String a bead on a headpin and make a plain loop. Open the loop and connect the link. Close the loop. Open an earring wire and connect the link. Close the earring wire. Make a second earring.

tip

These beads have a large hole, so the decorative end of the headpin keeps the beads in place. You can also string a small bead on a regular headpin for the same result.

Triple-dangle earrings

Materials

2 22mm links or large jump rings

2 6mm bicone beads

2 4mm bicone beads

4 4mm round beads

6 headpins

Pair of earring wires

1. String a 6mm bicone bead on a headpin and make a plain loop. String two 4mm round beads on a headpin and make a plain loop. String a 4mm bicone bead on a headpin and make a plain loop.

2. Open a loop above a dangle and connect the link. Repeat with two more beaded dangles.

3. Open an earring wire and connect the link. Close the earring wire.

4. Make a second earring.

another option

This pendant uses a 15mm link, a 3mm pearl, a 5mm flower bead with a 3mm spacer, and a 10mm rectangle gemstone with a 4mm round bead. The link is strung on a purchased necklace chain.

Big & little earrings

Materials

2 15mm oval beads

12 4mm round beads in three colors

12 headpins

4 in. (10cm) 20-gauge wire

Pair of earring wires

1. Cut a 2-in. (5cm) piece of wire. Working at the largest part of the roundnose pliers (nearest the handle), make a plain loop at one end.

2. String an oval bead and make a plain loop above the bead, working in the middle of the roundnose pliers.

3. String a 4mm bead on a headpin and make a plain loop above the bead, working at the tip of the roundnose pliers. Repeat to make six dangles in three colors.

4. Open the larger loop made in step 1 and attach the dangles made in step 3, alternating colors. Close the loop.

5. Open the smaller loop made in step 2 and attach an earring wire. Close the loop.

6. Make a second earring, stringing the dangles in reverse color order.

Make a wrapped loop

   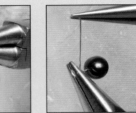 

▲ To make a wrapped loop above a bead, trim the wire about 1¼ in. (3.2cm) above the bead. Grasp the wire with chainnose pliers above the bead. Fold the wire over the pliers into a right-angle bend. If you're working with plain wire (no bead), grasp the wire about 1¼ in. down from the end and make a right-angle bend over the pliers.

▲ Switch to roundnose pliers, and position the jaws in the bend. Bring the end of the wire up and over the top jaw of the pliers, and as far down as you can.

▲ Reposition the roundnose pliers so the lower jaw is in the loop. Slide the wire down the shaft to be sure you are working in the same place as you did in step 2. Curve the wire downward around the bottom of the pliers until the tail is at a right angle to the stem. This is called "the first half of a wrapped loop." At this stage, you can add dangles or connect the loop to another element, such as a link of chain.

▲ To finish the wrapped loop, switch back to chainnose pliers. Position the pliers' jaw across the loop, as shown. Use a second pair of pliers—round-nose or chain-nose—to grasp the wire at the end and begin to wrap this piece around the exposed stem.

▲ One wrap will secure the loop, but several wraps look nicer. Be sure to fill in the entire gap between the loop and the bead so the bead is secure.

 tip **Changing where you work on the roundnose pliers changes the size of the loop.**

Statement bracelet

Materials

Finished length: silver bracelet 8 in. (20cm), copper bracelet 7½ in. (19.1cm)

15mm bead or charm

7 in. (18cm) large-link cable chain

3mm flat spacer (optional)

10mm beadcap

2-in. (5cm) headpin

2 7mm jump rings

Toggle clasp

1. Create a dangle: String the beadcap and the bead on the headpin, and add a spacer, if you like. Make a wrapped loop.

2. Open a jump ring and attach the dangle, one end of the chain, and the loop end of the toggle clasp. Close the jump ring.

3. Open a jump ring and attach the remaining end of the chain and the toggle end of the clasp. Close the jump ring.

 tip

If the hole in the beadcap or bead is larger than the head of the headpin, string a small spacer bead first, as in the copper bracelet.

Dainty dangle bracelet

Materials

Finished length: 7 in. (18cm)

6½-7½ in. (16.5–19.1cm) large cable chain

16–20 8mm pearls, crystals or a combination of both

16–20 2-in. (5cm) headpins

2 7mm jump rings

Lobster claw clasp

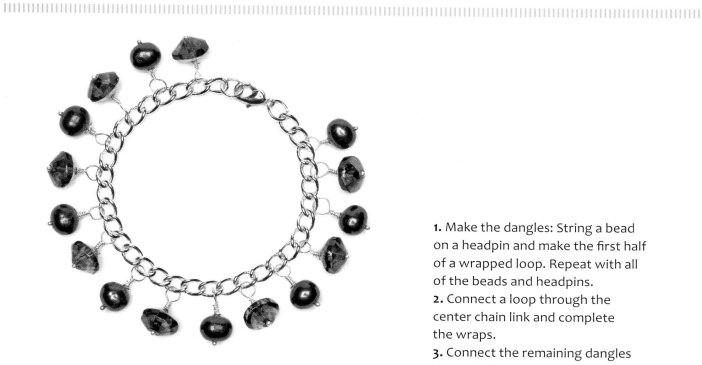

tip Work at the middle to larger part of the roundnose pliers to create a bigger loop. This will give your loops more swing.

1. Make the dangles: String a bead on a headpin and make the first half of a wrapped loop. Repeat with all of the beads and headpins.
2. Connect a loop through the center chain link and complete the wraps.
3. Connect the remaining dangles through the remaining links, skipping one link between each dangle. Check the fit as you get close to the end of the chain.
4. Connect a clasp to one chain end using a 7mm jump ring. Connect the remaining jump ring to the other chain end.

another option

Make a Lucite flower bracelet. This bracelet is made in the same way, but crystals, beads, and beadcaps are stacked on headpins in different combinations.

Overboard dangle bracelet

Materials

Finished length: 7¼ in. (18.4cm)

100–140 5mm lentil beads in two or three colors

15–20 dagger beads

15–20 charms

30–40 5–7mm jump rings

100–140 1½-in. (3.8cm) headpins

Pre-finished chain bracelet or 7½ in. (19.1cm) chain and clasp with jump ring

1. Create dangles: String two or three lentil beads on a headpin, and make the first half of a wrapped loop above the beads. Make two or three dangles for each link of chain.

2. Working from the center of the chain, attach a larger dangle to one side of a link and complete the wraps. Attach a smaller dangle to the other side of the link and complete the wraps. Continue attaching dangles, changing sides and sizes as you go, until you've attached two or three dangles to each link.

3. Open a jump ring. String a charm or a dagger. Connect the jump ring to a chain link and close the jump ring.

4. Repeat step 3 along the bracelet, attaching charms or daggers wherever you'd like. Attach the clasp to one end of the chain, if needed.

another option

When this bracelet is clasped, the burst of color reminds me of a wrist corsage. To make the bracelet: First, cut a length of chain to your desired bracelet length and attach a clasp half to each end with an 8mm heavy-gauge jump ring. Make 12–14 wrapped looped dangles using 4–8mm bicone crystals in several colors. Open a jump ring, string three or four dangles and a ring connecting a clasp half, and close the jump ring. Repeat to attach two sets of dangles to each end.

BASIC SKILL

Wrap above a top-drilled bead

▲ Cut a 3-in. (7cm) piece of wire, and center a top-drilled bead on the wire. Bend each side upward to form a squared-off U shape. Leave a tiny bit of room for the bead to move (about 1mm).

▲ Cross the wires into an X shape above the bead.

▲ Use chainnose pliers to bend one wire straight up and one wire to the side. They'll form a right angle at their intersection.

▲ Wrap the horizontal wire around the vertical wire as in a wrapped loop. Make two or three wraps, and trim the wire. At this point, you may make a plain or wrapped loop above the bead to create a dangle.

tip Briolettes often have small holes. Use thin wire, such as 22-gauge or 24-gauge, to fit through the hole.

tip String a tiny crystal or bead between the wraps made in the last step to help fill a potential gap and to add a bit of flash.

Dangle bangle bracelet

Materials

Purchased bangle bracelet

5–8mm gemstone briolette

5–8mm charm

5–6mm round crystal or gemstone bead

3 3mm jump rings or **1** 5mm jump ring

2-in. (5cm) headpin

3 in. (7.6cm) 20-gauge wire

1. String a crystal or gemstone bead on a headpin and make a wrapped loop above the bead.

2. String a briolette on the wire and wrap above the top-drilled bead. Make a wrapped loop with the remaining wire.

3. Use a 3mm jump ring to attach each dangle and the charm to the bangle bracelet.

4. Optional (middle bracelet): Open a 5mm jump ring and string the dangles, the charm, and the bangle. Close the jump ring. This keeps the charms clustered together.

Raindrop earrings

1. Cut the wire into two 3-in. (7.6cm) pieces. Using one wire, wrap above a top-drilled briolette.

2. String a crystal above the briolette. Make a plain loop above the crystal.

3. Cut the fine-link chain in half (see tip).

4. Open the loop and attach a briolette to one end of a chain. Close the loop.

5. Open an earring wire. Attach the other end of the chain. Close the earring wire.

6. Make a second earring.

Materials

2 10mm top-drilled briolette gemstones

2 2mm bicone crystals

2 in. (5cm) fine-link chain

6 in. (15cm) 22-gauge wire

Pair of earring wires

tip

To cut chain in half, string each end on a headpin or piece of wire. One link of chain should fall to the bottom. This is the center link; cut it for two even lengths of chain.

Waterfall earrings

Materials

10 briolette gemstones:
6 color A and **4** color B

2 6-link pieces of medium-link chain

2½ ft. (76cm) 22-gauge wire cut into **10** 3-in. (7.6cm) pieces

Pair of earring wires

1. Using 3-in. (7.6cm) pieces of wire, wrap above each top-drilled briolette.

2. With two color A briolettes, make the first half of a wrapped loop above each set of wraps.

3. Make a plain loop above the wraps of the remaining briolettes.

4. Attach a briolette from step 2 to the bottom link of a chain piece, and complete the wraps.

5. Alternating sides and colors, attach a briolette to every other link until you've attached four dangles.

6. Open an earring wire and string the remaining end link of chain. Close the earring wire.

7. Repeat steps 4–6 to finish the second earring.

Use crimps

FLATTEN A CRIMP

▲ Hold the crimp tube in the tip of chainnose pliers. Squeeze the pliers firmly to flatten the crimp.

▲ Tug the clasp to be sure the crimp has a solid grip.

USE A CRIMP COVER

▲ Place an open crimp cover over a folded crimp, and gently compress the cover with chainnose or crimping pliers.

MAKE A FOLDED CRIMP

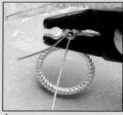  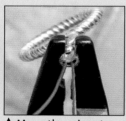 

▲ Position the crimp tube in the notch closest to the pliers' handle.

▲ Separate the wires, and firmly squeeze the crimp.

▲ Move the crimp to the notch at the pliers' tip, and squeeze the crimp tube, folding it in half at the indentation made in the previous step.

▲ Tug to be sure the crimp is secure.

tip

Choosing to use flat or folded crimps is a matter of preference. Flat crimps are easier to make. Folded crimps have a smaller profile and are more discreet. Folded crimps can be covered with a crimp cover.

Simple strung necklace

tip

Stringing a small bead on each side of the crimp tube creates a buffer, so the sometimes-sharp edge of the crimp tube is less likely to fray the wire against the clasp over time.

Materials

Finished length: 15 in. (38cm)

25–30 6–8mm rondelle beads

32–36 6mm round beads

2 crimp tubes

4 3mm round spacer beads

Toggle clasp

2 crimp covers (optional)

Flexible beading wire

1. Cut the flexible beading wire about 6 in. (15cm) longer than the desired length of your necklace. The extra length gives you a little flexibility in adjusting the fit of the necklace, and it makes it easier to bring the ends back through the crimp tubes. When you have more experience, you can reduce the extra length a bit.

2. Attach a bead stopper to one end of the wire.

3. String beads as desired. I strung an alternating pattern of rondelle beads and round beads.

4. On one end, string a 3mm spacer bead, a crimp tube, a spacer bead, and half of the clasp on the wire.

5. Bring the wire end back through the spacer bead, the crimp tube, and the spacer bead. Pull the wire through, creating a small loop.

6. Grasp the crimp tube with chainnose pliers and squeeze gently to flatten, or use crimping pliers to make a folded crimp.

7. Repeat step 4 on the other end, removing the bead stopper and using the remaining clasp half. Bring the wire through the beads just strung. Tighten the wire and check the fit. Then add or remove beads to adjust the fit as needed. Grasp the crimp tube with chainnose pliers and flatten, or use crimping pliers to make a folded crimp.

8. Trim the excess wire from each end.

9. Open a crimp cover and place it over the folded crimp. Gently close the crimp cover. Repeat on the other end.

Multistrand necklace with slide clasp

Materials

Finished length: 16 in. (41cm) shortest strand, 17½ in. (44.5cm) longest strand

71 8mm Czech glass round beads

22 8mm gemstone beads

35 4mm round beads

99 4mm gemstone beads

6 crimp tubes

3-strand slide clasp

Flexible beading wire

tip Check the fit, and add or remove beads to get the fit you desire. This necklace appears to be three equal-length strands when worn. If you'd like more drape and space between your strands, increase the difference in length between the strands in step 2.

tip Close the slide clasp before you crimp. It's easy to get the orientation mixed up if you work with each half separately.

1. Cut three strands of beading wire 6 in. (15cm) longer than your desired finished length.

2. Place a bead stopper at the end of each wire. String beads as desired. String strand #1 to your desired length for the shortest strand, allowing about ½ in. (1.3cm) for the clasp. String strand #2 ½–¾ in. (1.3–1.9cm) longer than strand #1. String strand #3 ½–¾ in. longer than strand #2. (My strands are 17¾ in./45.1cm, 17 in./43cm, and 16¼ in./41.3cm long.)

3. Close the slide clasp. At one end of strand #2, remove the bead stopper. String a 4mm bead, a crimp tube, a 4mm bead, and the middle loop of half the clasp. Go back through the beads just strung, and pull the end tight. Make a folded crimp. Repeat with the other end and the middle loop of the remaining clasp half, checking the fit before you make the folded crimp.

4. Repeat step 3 with the remaining strands, checking the fit before you make the final crimp each time. Trim all the excess wires.

Illusion necklace

1. Cut the flexible beading wire into three pieces: 16 in. (41cm), 18 in. (46cm), and 20 in. (51cm).
2. On the longest strand, string a crimp tube. String a pearl and two crimp tubes. Repeat until you have 16 pearls, and then string one crimp tube (32 crimps total).
3. Make a folded crimp 2 in. (5cm) from the end of the wire. Slide a pearl and a crimp tube snug to the folded crimp, and make a folded crimp with the second tube. Continue crimping pearls in place, leaving about an inch between each one. Don't worry if your spacing isn't perfect—you just want an open and airy look.
4. Repeat steps 2 and 3 with the 18-in. strand, stringing 12 pearls and 24 crimp tubes. Begin the first crimp 3 in. (7.6cm) from the end.
5. Repeat step 4 with the shortest strand, but make the first crimp 1½ in. (3.8cm) from the end.
6. Gather the strands together and even them up on one end. Apply superglue, and insert the strands into a crimp end. Flatten the middle of the crimp end to tighten.
7. Repeat step 6 on the other end.
8. Use the 3mm jump ring to attach the clasp. Attach the 7mm jump ring on the other end.

 Micro crimp tubes (1.1x1mm) provide a more discreet finish to this necklace, but they also require a special pair of pliers. I used standard crimps so you don't have to buy another tool.

Materials

Finished length: 16½ in. (41.9cm) shortest strand, 20 in. (51cm) longest strand

40 pearls in different colors and shapes (keishi and potato pearls in **3** colors)

80 crimp tubes

2 crimp ends

Lobster claw clasp

3mm jump ring

7mm jump ring

Flexible beading wire (SoftFlex 925 Sterling Silver)

Superglue

tip **By using crimps you can create the "illusion" that these pearls are floating around your neck. Choose a treated flexible beading wire—they come in many colors as well as metallics, including silver and gold.**

BASIC SKILL
Make knots

SURGEON'S KNOT

▲ Cross the right end over the left end and go under and over the cord. Go over and under again.

▲ Cross the left end over the right end and go through once. Pull the ends to tighten the knot. Optional, glue the knot with a flexible glue such as G-S Hypo Cement.

OVERHAND KNOT

▲ Make a loop and pass the working ends through it. Pull the ends to tighten the knot.

LARK'S HEAD KNOT

▲ Fold a cord in half and lay it behind a ring, loop, etc. with the fold pointing down. Bring the ends through the ring from back to front, then through the fold, and tighten.

KNOT BEADS

▲ Make an overhand knot on a cord. String a bead, and snug the bead up next to the knot. Make an overhand knot as close to the bead as you can, using a sturdy piece of wire or the tips of roundnose pliers to guide the knot. Pull the knot tight.

Skinny stretchy stacks

Materials

**Finished length:
approximately 7 in. (18cm)**

65 (approximately) 2–3mm
beads or 11º–6º seed beads

0.13 diameter ribbon elastic

Flexible eye needle

G-S Hypo Cement

Crimp cover (optional)

Tape

1. Cut elastic to twice your desired length plus 6 in. (15cm).
2. Center the needle on the elastic, and tape the ends.
3. String 7 in. (18cm) of beads and check the fit. Add or remove beads if necessary.
4. Tie a surgeon's knot, trim the ends, and dab the knot with glue. A flexible glue, such as G-S Hypo Cement, works with elastic.
5. Slide the knot into a bead or cover with a crimp cover.

 For an alternating bead pattern, begin with color A and end with color B so the pattern is continuous when the knot is tied.

Connected stacks

Materials

Finished length: 7 in. (18cm)

15mm large-hole bead

150 3mm round beads

0.13 diameter ribbon elastic

Flexible eye needle

G-S Hypo Cement

Tape

1. Cut elastic to twice your desired length plus 6 in. (15cm). Center the needle on the elastic, and tape the ends.
2. String 7 in. (18cm) of beads and check the fit. Add or remove beads if necessary.
3. Pass the beaded strand through the 15mm bead.
4. Remove the tape and trim the end to remove the needle. Tie a surgeon's knot (with two pieces of elastic on each side), trim the ends, and dab the knot with glue.
5. Slide the knot into the 15mm bead.
6. Repeat steps 1–5 with two additional beaded strands.

tip **Big beads take up more space, so your bracelet will have to be a bit longer than it would with smaller beads. Check the fit carefully in step 4 before you knot the elastic.**

Celebration bracelet

1. String a crystal on a headpin and make a wrapped loop. Repeat with all the crystals.
2. Cut a 24-in. (61cm) piece of ribbon elastic. Center the needle and tape the ends.
3. String a 17mm bead, a color A dangle, a color B dangle, a color C dangle, an A, a B, and a C.
4. Repeat step 3 eight times. Check the fit. Add or remove a full set of the pattern, if necessary.
5. Tie a surgeon's knot and glue the knot. Slide the knot into the hole of a 17mm bead.

Materials

Finished length: approximately 8 in. (20cm)

9–10 17mm round beads

54–60 6mm bicone crystals in 3 colors: A, B, and C

54–60 ball-tipped headpins

0.13 diameter ribbon elastic

Flexible eye needle

G-S Hypo Cement

Tape

Knotted bead wrap bracelet

Materials

Finished length: 27 in. (69cm) for a four-wrap bracelet

1½ yd. (1.4m) 3mm suede cord

13–15 large-hole gemstone beads or pearls

2 3mm crimp ends

2 5–7mm jump rings

Lobster claw clasp

GS Hypo Cement

1. Tie an overhand knot about 3 in. (7.6cm) from one end of the suede cord.

2. String a pearl or gemstone bead, and snug it next to the knot.

3. Tie an overhand knot as close as possible to the bead.

4. Repeat until the beaded section is about 21 in. (53cm) long. Space the knots and beads about 1 in. (2.5cm) apart. This does not have to be exact.

5. Check the fit (the bracelet should wrap around your wrist three or four times). Mark the cord ends where you'd like them to meet, allowing about 1 in. for the clasp. Trim the cord ends to the mark.

6. Apply a dab of glue to one end of the cord, and place it in a crimp end. Flatten the crimp end with chainnose pliers. Repeat on the other end.

7. Attach a jump ring and the clasp to one end, and attach a jump ring to the other end.

tip **The crimp end used on the orange bracelet is designed to be used as the loop of the hook-and-loop clasp.**

tip **Gluing the crimp end provides security, especially for a bracelet, which gets a lot of action when worn.**

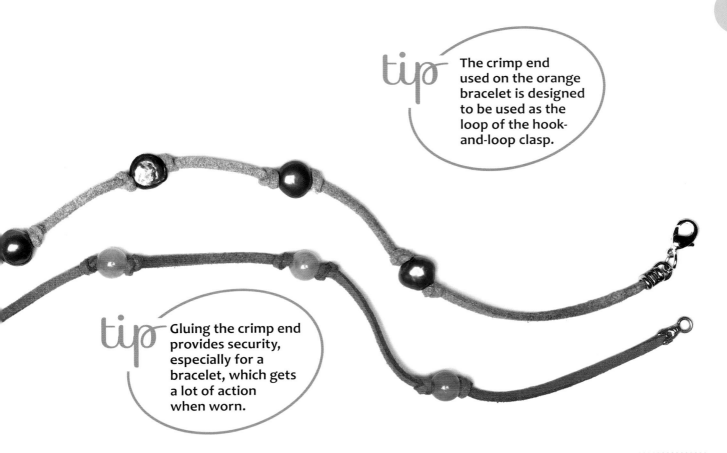

Multistrand open knotted necklace

Materials

Finished length: 20 in. (51cm)

30 10mm acrylic beads

2 4mm round beads

5 1-yd. (.9m) pieces of hemp cord

2 2mm cones

2 7mm jump rings

2 6-in. (15cm) pieces of 20-gauge wire

Toggle clasp

1. Make an overhand knot about 3 in. (7.6cm) from one end of a piece of hemp cord.

2. String a 10mm bead, and snug it up next to the knot. Make an overhand knot as close to the bead as you can. Use a sturdy piece of wire or the tips of your roundnose pliers to guide the knot. Pull the knot tight.

3. Repeat to string and knot six beads about 1–1½ in. (2.5–3.8cm) apart.

4. Repeat steps 1–3 on each piece of hemp, staggering the bead placement slightly from cord to cord.

5. Check the fit of the necklace. Trim the ends of the hemp so the necklace is about 1 in. shorter than your desired length.

6. With roundnose pliers, make a small hook at one end of a piece of wire. On one side, gather all the cord ends and hook the wire around the bundle. Wrap the wire around the cords three or four times **(photo a)**.

7. With chainnose pliers, make a bend in the wire so it is parallel to the cords **(photo b)**. String a cone and a 4mm bead. Make a wrapped loop above the bead **(photo c)**.

9. Repeat steps 6 and 7 on the other end of the necklace.

10. Use a jump ring to attach a clasp half to each loop.

tip Group several beads between knots instead of just one for a variation of this style.

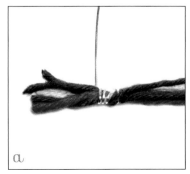

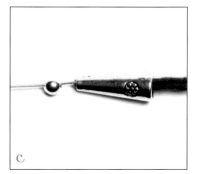

Knotted big bead necklace

Materials

Finished length: 18 in. (46cm)

28–30 12mm round beads

32 in. (81cm) linen cord

6 in. (15cm) 22-gauge wire (optional)

Lobster claw clasp and closed ring

1. Tie an overhand knot 3 in. (7.6cm) from the cord end.

2. String a round bead and push it to the knot.

3. Tie an overhand knot and use a sturdy piece of wire, plier tips, or an awl to guide the knot to the bead. Pull the knot tight.

4. Repeat steps 2 and 3 with the remaining beads until the necklace is the desired length.

5. On one end, string the clasp and tie an overhand knot about ¼ in. (6mm) from the last knot. Repeat on the other end with the closed ring.

6. Optional: Cut 3 in. of wire. Hold the cord tail next to the necklace cord, and wrap the wire over the two cords until you reach the last knot. Repeat on the other end.

Brass ring necklace

Materials

Finished length: 19 in. (48cm)

30mm ring

2 crimp ends

2 5–7mm jump rings

Lobster claw clasp

20 in. (51cm) ⅛-in. (3mm) suede lace

G-S Hypo Cement

1. Fold the suede lace in half, and tie a lark's head knot around the ring.
2. Dab a lace end with glue and insert it into each crimp end. Repeat with the other end.
3. Use chainnose pliers to flatten the middle of the crimp end.
4. Open a jump ring. Pick up the clasp and one crimp end. Close the jump ring.
5. Attach a jump ring to the remaining crimp end.

other options

Fold a 40-in. (1m) silk ribbon in half. Make a lark's head knot around a 30mm gemstone donut. Wear the necklace by tying a bow with the ribbon ends. You can also cut a 20-in. (51cm) piece of fine chain. Fold the chain in half, and make a lark's head knot around a 30mm oval crystal ring. Check the fit and cut the chain if necessary. Use jump rings to attach a clasp half to each end of the chain.

Center ring bracelet

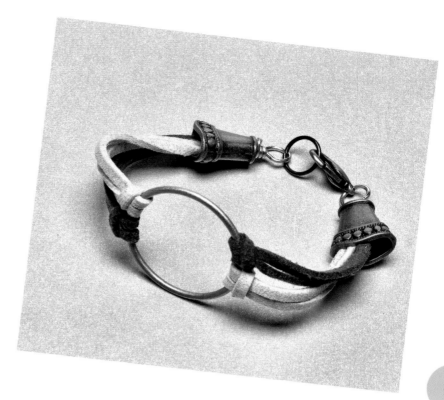

Materials

Finished length: 7 in. (18cm)

25mm ring

12 in. (30cm) suede cord in each of **2** colors: A and B

2 15mm cones

Lobster claw clasp and jump ring

6 in. (15cm) 22-gauge wire

1. Cut the suede into four 6-in. (15cm) pieces.
2. Tie a lark's head knot around the ring with a color A cord. Repeat with a color B cord. On the other side of the ring, repeat with the remaining cord, alternating the placement of the colors.
3. Check the fit and trim the suede ends, allowing 1 in. (2.5cm) on each side for the clasp.
4. Cut a 3-in. (7.6cm) piece of wire. Wrap the suede ends with three or four wraps. Extend the wire perpendicular to the wraps.
5. String a cone and make a wrapped loop with the wire end. Attach the clasp to the loop before you complete the wraps. Repeat on the other end with the jump ring.

Linen and loop fringe earrings

Materials

12 6º seed beads, **4** color A and **8** color B

1 yd. (.9m) linen cord

30–35mm purchased hoop earrings

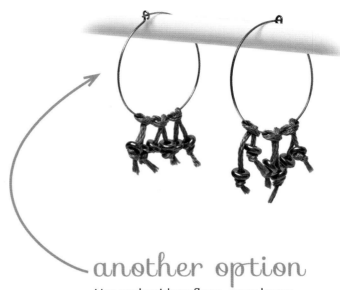

another option

Use embroidery floss, 4mm brass heishi beads, and 10mm diameter hoop earrings for this smaller version.

1. Cut a 5-in. (13cm) piece of linen cord (you will have some waste, but it's easier to tie the knots with a longer length of cord). Fold the cord in half, and make a lark's head knot around the hoop earring.

2. String a color A seed bead on one cord end. Tie an overhand knot about ½ in. (1.3cm) from the lark's head knot. Repeat with the second cord end. Trim the extra cord.

3. Repeat steps 1 and 2 on each side using color B seed beads and tying the overhand knots about ⅜ in. (1cm) from the lark's head knot.

4. Repeat steps 1–3 to make a second earring. Watch the orientation of the earring — when you wear the pair, you want the "bumps" facing out on each.

Don't overthink, overplan, or overexecute. Don't try to have one piece do it all. A stack of eight beads on a headpin is about four too many for a pretty earring. Limit the materials or the techniques to keep your project from becoming overwhelming or over executed. The projects that follow in this section give you lots of tips and tricks for working with bold materials in a refined way. I have a favorite saying: "Just because you can, doesn't always mean you should."

Keep it Simple

The jewelry you make is not a walking portfolio of your skills. Rather, your skills will shine through when your piece has perfect drape, balance, and color.

2

DESIGN SKILL

Spacers and beadcaps

Big beads are beautiful, but they can give a heavy look to a necklace. Using spacer beads (small beads like seed beads, flat disk or flower shaped spacers, or round 3mm beads) and beadcaps can bring balance and pacing to a plain design. Here are three options that illustrate how well-placed spacer beads can bring elegance or whimsy to a big-bead necklace.

Light and lively necklace

Materials

Finished length: 15½ in. (39.4cm)

3 15mm round pearls

4 8mm flat spacers

Flexible beading wire (silver plated)

2 crimp tubes

Lobster claw clasp and 5mm soldered jump ring

1. Cut the flexible beading wire about 6 in. (15cm) longer than the desired length of your necklace.
2. String a round bead, two spacers, a round bead, two spacers, and a round bead.
3. On one end, string a crimp tube and a lobster claw clasp. Come back through the crimp tube. Make a folded crimp, and trim the wire end.
4. On the other end, string a crimp tube and a soldered ring. Come back through the crimp tube and check the fit. Adjust, if needed.
5. Make a folded crimp and trim the wire end.

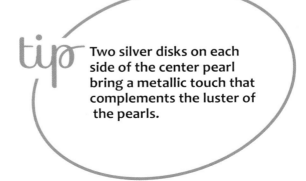

tip Two silver disks on each side of the center pearl bring a metallic touch that complements the luster of the pearls.

Gumball necklace

1. Cut the flexible beading wire about 6 in. (15cm) longer than the desired length of your necklace.

2. String a flat spacer, a beadcap, a 15mm bead, and a beadcap. Repeat until you have reached the desired length, and end with a spacer.

3. On each end, string a crimp tube and half of the clasp. Go back through the crimp tube and check the fit. Adjust, if needed.

4. On each end, make a folded crimp and trim the wire. Close a crimp cover over the crimp.

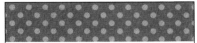

Materials

Finished length: 17 in. (43cm)

22 15mm round beads

23 3mm flat spacers

44 7x4mm flower filigree beadcaps

Flexible beading wire

2 crimp tubes

2 crimp covers

Lobster claw clasp and soldered jump ring

61

another option

Delicate flower-shaped filigree beadcaps work in the turquoise necklace, but heavier copper caps hug these oversized pearls without overshadowing them. Each option gives a much airier and balanced look than just stringing the beads alone. A tiny, flat spacer between each set gives added dimension to the design.

Jawbreaker necklace

Materials

Finished length: 20 in. (51cm)

3 25mm round beads

4 3mm round beads

2 crimp tubes

2 crimp covers

Flexible beading wire

16-in. open-link chain, cut into two 8-in. (20cm) pieces

7mm jump ring

Lobster claw clasp

1. Cut an 8-in. (20cm) piece of flexible beading wire.
2. String a 3mm round bead, a 25mm round bead, a 3mm, a 25mm, a 3mm, a 25mm, and a 3mm.
3. On each end, string a crimp tube and one end of a chain piece. Go back through the crimp tube, and make a folded crimp. Trim the wire. Attach a crimp cover over the crimp.
4. On one end, attach the lobster claw clasp to the chain with the 7mm jump ring.

tip

Between the bright color and the giant size, these green faux-Lucite beads are irresistible. Tiny blue spacer beads act as bumpers between the big beads, and an open, airy chain keeps the design light and comfortable to wear.

Pacer beads

It's not an official beading term, but I like to use small beads (3–4mm round or bicone) or larger 6º or 8º seed beads to "pace" a necklace or bracelet. I find that the bigger beads are nicely framed by the smaller beads.

DO group pacer beads in odd numbers. It's an age-old design trick that really works.

DO use seed beads as pacer beads. Larger seed beads create a wonderful effect, they come in many colors and finishes, and they are an inexpensive and easy-to-find material.

DO think about bead shape. Pacer beads don't have to be round. Tiny bicone crystals or peanut-shaped seed beads add texture as well as balance.

DON'T overdo it. Remember, pacer beads are the backdrop—like a canvas. The main beads in your design are the focus, and should shine through.

Black and
silver necklace

1. Cut two pieces of beading wire 6 in. (15cm) longer than the desired length of your necklace.

2. On one wire, string a pattern of large and small beads. Follow the pattern in the project, or create your own.

3. On the second wire, string a pattern of small beads. Make this strand 1 in. (2.5cm) shorter than the first strand.

4. On one end of each wire, string a 3mm spacer bead, a crimp tube, a spacer, and one loop of half of the clasp. Come back through the beads just strung.

5. Repeat step 4 on the other end of the necklace. Check the fit, and add or remove beads if needed.

6. Crimp the crimp tubes and trim the wire ends.

Materials

Finished length: 17/19 in. (43/48cm)

9 15mm oval beads

57 5mm round beads

151 4mm round beads

8 3mm round spacer beads

4 crimp tubes

2-strand clasp

Flexible beading wire

65

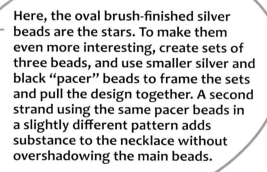

tip

Here, the oval brush-finished silver beads are the stars. To make them even more interesting, create sets of three beads, and use smaller silver and black "pacer" beads to frame the sets and pull the design together. A second strand using the same pacer beads in a slightly different pattern adds substance to the necklace without overshadowing the main beads.

Garden party necklace

Even large Lucite beads are lightweight. A necklace this long made from gemstones and metal might be uncomfortable to wear.

Materials

Finished length 39 in. (.99m)

Lucite beads

- **10** 15mm round pearl

- **11** 10mm round

- **20** 8mm round

- **27** 6mm round

- **23** 5mm round

- **13** 9x12mm rondelle beads

- **2** 15mm lilies

- **8** leaf-shaped beadcaps

38 4mm bicone crystals in several colors

22 3mm bicone crystals in several colors

2 crimp tubes

Lobster claw clasp and ring

Flexible beading wire

note: **All quantities are estimates. Choose beads you like in similar sizes and in quantities to provide the length you desire.**

To string the necklace, create patterns of beads in 1–3 in. (2.5–7.6cm) segments. String each set, and frame the set with crystal "pacer beads." As you pass the center point, think about how sets of beads will line up on each side of the necklace. I prefer to have similar sets on each side, but not a true mirror image. Attach the clasp after you've strung beads to your desired length.

This necklace is all about color and fun. The oversized Lucite "pearls" make a statement, but the Lucite alone would have been simultaneously too much and not enough. Strategic use of pacer beads (5mm Lucite rounds and 3mm and 4mm bicone crystals) opens up this design. Pacer beads give the piece an airy feel and accent the bold colors of the main beads without making the necklace heavy or dense.

Wrap necklace
or bracelet

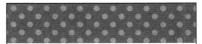

Materials

Finished length: 56 in. (1.42m)

7 6mm round beads

47 4mm round beads

55 3mm round beads

25 5mm square beads, diagonal hole

55 4mm heishi beads

27 3mm heishi beads

1 g triangle beads

2–4 g (approximately) farfalle (peanut) seed beads in **2** colors

2 crimp tubes

Lobster claw clasp and ring

Flexible beading wire

1. Determine your finished length: Measure your wrist first, and multiply by eight. Check to see that this length will also work as a three-strand necklace. Add about 6 in. (15cm), and cut the beading wire to this length.

2. Create mini patterns of beads (mine are equal to about half my wrist measurement), and string until you've reached your desired length.

3. Crimp a clasp half to each end.

69

Inspired by the beads in the "Skinny Stretchy Stacks" bracelets, p. 43, this beaded necklace can be worn as a super long strand, knotted flapper-style in front, draped as a three-strand princess-length adornment, or wrapped eight times around your wrist. The combinations and patterns create the pacing in this necklace.

Multistrand options

Creating a multistrand necklace can often be challenging for new beaders, but the look is great. Here are a few things to keep in mind:

DO use the same accent or "pacer" beads in each strand to give the necklace continuity.

DO use the biggest beads in the longest strand.

DO choose a clasp designed for multiple strands.

DO check the fit before crimping or finishing. "Measure twice, cut once" is the mantra for multistrands.

DON'T overcrowd or overexecute your design.

Easy multistrand look

tip

You've heard the expression, "fake it 'til you make it," right? An easy way to get a multistrand look is to make three necklaces in different lengths and wear them at the same time. Shh...don't tell. Here, I've used seed bead mixes to create three complementary strands. Add a few charms to personalize your necklaces and emphasize the layered look.

tip Use a soldered or closed jump ring to finish the necklace. It prevents the flexible beading wire from sliding through the opening in a traditional jump ring when the necklace is worn.

1. Cut a piece of beading wire to the desired length of your first necklace.
2. String seed beads in a pattern of your choice. Try using repeating groups of three and five beads.
3. On each end, string a crimp tube, a seed bead, and a soldered jump ring. Come back through the crimp tube and a few seed beads. Tighten the wire, and check the fit. Add or remove beads if needed. Crimp the crimp tubes, and trim the excess wire.
4. On one end, attach the spring clasp with a 3mm jump ring.
5. Open a 7mm jump ring, string a charm and the necklace, and close the jump ring.
6. Repeat steps 1–5 twice to finish each strand of the necklace, making them about 1–2 in. (2.5–5cm) different in length.

Materials

Finished lengths: 16 in. (41cm), 18 in. (46cm), and 19 in. (48cm)

11º–6º seed beads in several colors (try a pre-mixed assortment from a craft store)

3 15mm charms (Nunn Design, nunndesign.com)

3 7mm open jump rings

6 5mm soldered jump rings

3 5mm open jump rings

3 spring clasps

6 crimp tubes

Flexible beading wire

tip A lightweight clasp, like a spring clasp, will stay in place when the necklace is worn. A heavier clasp may "travel" to the front.

Three-strand bracelet

Materials

Finished length: 8 in. (20cm)

14 in. (36cm) large-link chain, silver

7 in. (18cm) large-link chain, gold

2–4 12mm jump rings

Lobster claw clasp and ring

73

1. Cut three pieces of chain to your desired bracelet length, allowing about 1 in. (2.5cm) for the clasp. My chains are 6¾ in. (17.1cm) long because my clasp is oversized.

2. Open a 12mm jump ring, and attach three chain ends and a clasp half. Close the jump ring. Repeat with a second jump ring for a stronger connection.

3. Repeat step 3 on the other end with the remaining clasp half or ring.

Half & half chain and beaded necklace

Materials

Finished length: 17½/18½ in. (44.5/47cm)

36 6mm round beads in **2** colors: **21** color A and **15** color B

24 6mm spacers

19 in. (48cm) double-link chain

6 8mm jump rings

4 crimp tubes

Lobster claw clasp

Flexible beading wire

tip Combining a beaded section with chain makes for a comfortable fit, especially if the beads are heavy or large. Using chain also is an easy way to control the strand lengths, since it's easier to snip a few links than it is to restring your beads.

1. Cut a 12-in. (30cm) piece of beading wire and string a pattern of 15 beads and 12 spacers.

2. Cut a 13-in (33cm) piece of beading wire and string a pattern of 21 beads and 12 spacers.

3. Cut the chain into two 5-in. (13cm) pieces and two 4¾-in. (12.1cm) pieces.

4. On one end of the shorter beaded strand, string a crimp tube and the end links of the 4¾-in. chain. Come back through a few beads and make a folded crimp. Repeat on the other end with the remaining 4¾-in. chain.

5. Repeat step 4 with the longer beaded strand and the 5-in. chain pieces.

6. On one end, use two 8mm jump rings to connect the two chain pieces. Repeat on the other end.

7. On one end, attach a clasp with an 8mm jump ring going through the two rings attached in step 6. Repeat on the other end with a single jump ring.

tip Use two jump rings together in step 6 to mimic the look of the chain. If your chain is different than mine, use a single jump ring.

Let the Materials Tell the Story

3

A beautiful focal bead or pendant needs a simple backdrop. Plain beads might look better clustered together. Bright colors need neutral connections. Properly planned, your jewelry will speak for itself. Projects in this chapter are more "show" than "tell." Now that you know the basics, you'll be able to string the designs without the detailed instruction given in the previous chapters.

Center the focal bead

You go to a bead show and become enamored with glorious gemstones or handcrafted art beads—but you become paralyzed, not knowing what to do with such a statement piece. Sound familiar? It's a common dilemma. Here are some options for taking a focal bead and making a beautiful backdrop.

DO let the focal bead take center stage. Choose accent beads that complement the focal, not overwhelm it.

DO keep it simple. A repeating pattern with two or three beads is all you need.

DO add a pop of color. Try to reflect the colors in the pendant and tie the design together.

DO keep the length to about 16 in. (41cm). The focal bead should nestle just under the base of your clavicle for a comfortable fit.

DON'T over-embellish the focal. All you need to do is to frame it with spacer beads or a decorative headpin to hide the hole.

Bold focal x 2

Materials

Finished length: 16½ in. (41.9cm)

35mm round gemstone
focal bead

30 6mm round beads

42 4mm round gemstone
beads: **36** in color A and
6 in color B

6 3mm flat spacer beads

Lobster claw clasp and ring

2 crimp tubes

Flexible beading wire

1. Cut a piece of flexible beading wire to
6 in. (15cm) longer than your desired length.
Center a focal bead on the wire.

2. On each side, string a flat spacer.

3. On each side, string a 4mm color A bead
and a 6mm round bead. Repeat nine times.
String a color A bead.

4. On each side, string a 4mm color B bead
and a flat spacer. Repeat for a total of three
beads and two spacers.

5. String an alternating pattern of color A
beads and 6mm rounds until the necklace is
the desired length.

6. On each end, string a crimp bead, a 4mm
round bead, and half the clasp. Go back
through the beads just strung and tighten
the wire. Check the fit. Add or remove beads
if necessary.

7. Crimp the crimp beads and trim the
excess wire.

Black and silver focal

tip

The two obvious options
when working with a center-
drilled focal bead are to string
it horizontally on beading
wire, as in this necklace, or to
create a pendant by stringing
it on a headpin and making
a wrapped loop, as in the
project on the next page.

Materials

Finished length: 16 in. (41cm) with 1¾ in. (4.4cm) dangle

35mm round gemstone focal bead

26 10mm round gemstone beads

60 4mm flat spacer beads

3-in. (7.6cm) decorative headpin

Lobster claw clasp and ring

2 crimp beads

Flexible beading wire

Copper and gemstone focal

1. String a 35mm round gemstone on the headpin and make a wrapped loop above the bead.

2. Cut a piece of flexible beading wire 6 in. (15cm) longer than your desired length.

3. Center the dangle on the beading wire.

4. On each side, string two spacers and a 10mm round. Repeat the pattern until the necklace is the desired length.

5. On each end, string two spacers, a crimp bead, two spacers, and half the clasp.

6. Go back through the beads just strung and tighten the wire. Check the fit. Add or remove beads if necessary.

7. Crimp the crimp beads and trim the extra wire.

House of whimsy

Materials

**Necklace finished length:
17 in. (43cm) with 1½ in. (3.8cm) dangle**

House focal bead (Heather Powers, humblebeads.com)

4 5x12mm polymer clay disk beads (Heather Powers)

6 10mm round gemstone beads in **2** colors

20 6⁰ Czech glass seed beads

2 crimp tubes

10 in. (25cm) double-length chain

2 5mm jump rings

Clasp

Flexible beading wire

**Bracelet finished length:
7 in. (18cm)**

House focal bead (Heather Powers)

6 5x12mm polymer clay disk beads (Heather Powers)

8 6mm faceted rondelle gemstones

18 6⁰ Czech glass seed beads

2 crimp tubes

Toggle clasp

Flexible beading wire

This jewelry takes it design cue from the polymer clay house bead and complementary disk beads, made by artist Heather Powers (humblebeads.com). I chose white accent beads to reflect the white in the focal bead. For the bracelet, the tree agate faceted rondelles have the perfect swirl of green on white to mimic the design in the disk beads and add a touch of unifying color. The necklace features round cracked agate beads in rich colors. To keep the necklace from being too serious, I used different gemstone colors on each side and finished the back with chain. A full beaded strand would have made the necklace bulky—counter to the whimsical and light look I was after.

Necklace

1. On a ball-tipped headpin, string a flat spacer, a 6⁰ seed bead, and a house bead. Make a wrapped loop above the beads.
2. Cut a 10-in. piece of flexible beading wire. Cut the chain into two 5-in. lengths.
3. Center the pendant on the wire.
4. On each end, string three 6⁰ seed beads.
5. On each end, string a gemstone, a seed bead, a polymer disk, and a seed bead. Repeat once.
6. On each end, string a seed bead, a crimp tube, a seed bead, and an end link of chain. Go back through the beads just strung. Crimp the crimp tubes and trim the excess wire.
7. On each end of the chain, attach a clasp half with a jump ring.

Bracelet

1. Cut a 10-in. piece of flexible beading wire. Center the house bead on the wire.
2. On each end, string beads as shown. Use the gemstones and seed beads to pace the design.
3. On each end, string a seed bead, a crimp tube, a seed bead, and half the clasp. Go back through the beads just strung and check the fit. Add or remove beads if necessary. Crimp the crimp tubes and trim the excess wire.

DESIGN SKILL

Asymmetry

An asymmetrical placement is the neon arrow of jewelry design—it calls more attention to your lovely find than a center placement might. Keeping a few tips in mind, you can master the asymmetrical approach.

DO measure from the top of your collarbone to where you'd like the center of the necklace to fall. Create your accent pattern to fit this length — usually it's about 3–5 in. (7.6–13cm).

DO pick subtle accent or pacer beads for the remainder of the necklace. Remember, you're framing your focal, not overwhelming it.

DO counterbalance the necklace with a substantial clasp. You don't want gravity to make the necklace twist and turn.

DON'T overdo the pattern. Keep two-thirds of the necklace in the background, and let one-third be the shining star.

Asymmetrical necklace

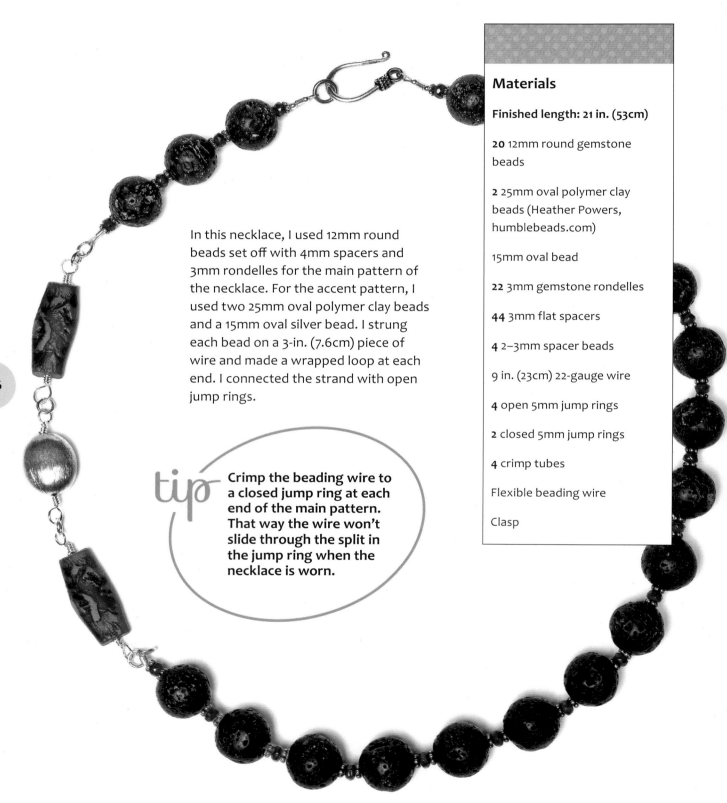

In this necklace, I used 12mm round beads set off with 4mm spacers and 3mm rondelles for the main pattern of the necklace. For the accent pattern, I used two 25mm oval polymer clay beads and a 15mm oval silver bead. I strung each bead on a 3-in. (7.6cm) piece of wire and made a wrapped loop at each end. I connected the strand with open jump rings.

tip Crimp the beading wire to a closed jump ring at each end of the main pattern. That way the wire won't slide through the split in the jump ring when the necklace is worn.

Materials

Finished length: 21 in. (53cm)

20 12mm round gemstone beads

2 25mm oval polymer clay beads (Heather Powers, humblebeads.com)

15mm oval bead

22 3mm gemstone rondelles

44 3mm flat spacers

4 2–3mm spacer beads

9 in. (23cm) 22-gauge wire

4 open 5mm jump rings

2 closed 5mm jump rings

4 crimp tubes

Flexible beading wire

Clasp

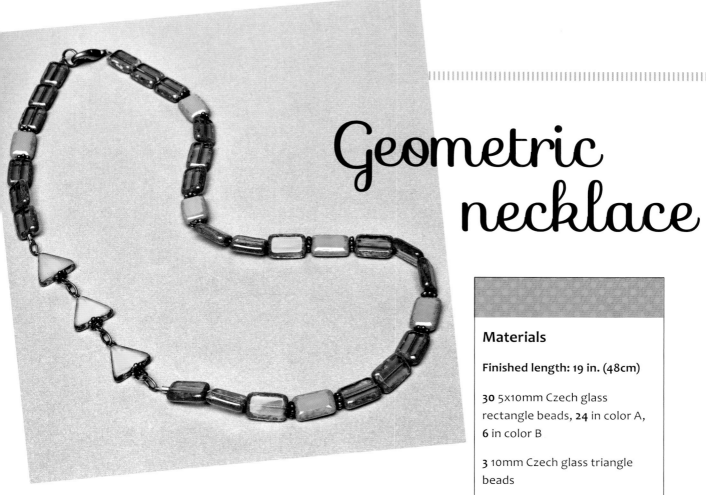

Geometric necklace

Materials

Finished length: 19 in. (48cm)

30 5x10mm Czech glass rectangle beads, **24** in color A, **6** in color B

3 10mm Czech glass triangle beads

15 4mm flat spacers

3 2-in. (5cm) headpins or 6 in. (15cm) 22-gauge wire

4 oval jump rings

4 crimp tubes

Flexible beading wire

Clasp and ring

1. Trim the end from a headpin or cut a 2-in. (5cm) piece of wire. Make a plain loop at one end, and string a spacer and a triangle. Make a plain loop above the beads. Repeat to make three triangle links.

2. Use oval jump rings to connect the triangle links into a chain. Attach an oval jump ring to the loop on each end of the chain.

3. Cut a 16-in. (41cm) piece of beading wire. String a pattern of three color A rectangles, a spacer, a color B rectangle, and a spacer for approximately 12 in. (30cm).

4. Cut an 8-in. (20cm) piece of beading wire. Repeat the pattern in step 3 for 3½ in. (8.9cm).

5. On the shorter strand, string a crimp tube and the end loop of the "top" of the beaded chain. Come back through a few beads and crimp the crimp tube. Crimp the loop end of the clasp to the other end of this strand.

6. Repeat step 5 with the longer beaded strand, crimping one end to the remaining end of the chain and one end to the clasp. Check the fit and the drape of the necklace before you make the final crimp, and add or remove beads if needed.

If you don't have soldered jump rings, use oval rings. The split is in the side, so gravity works in your favor and keeps the flexible beading wire against the solid edge of the oval.

Eclectic bracelet

Materials

Finished length: 7½ in. (19.1cm)

20mm wavy flat gemstone oval

3 5x12mm polymer clay disk beads (Heather Powers, humblebeads.com)

5 6mm wooden beads

6mm round crystal

6mm flower

7 10mm flat shell spacers

4mm spacer

19 3mm round beads

4 11º seed beads

3-in. (7.6cm) decorative headpin

2 crimp tubes

Lobster claw clasp and ring

Flexible beading wire

1. String the 4mm spacer and the flower on the headpin. Make a wrapped loop above the beads.
2. Cut a piece of flexible beading wire to a few inches longer than your desired length.
3. String the beads, using the 3mm rounds to pace the design.
4. On one end, string an 11º, a crimp tube, an 11º, and the lobster claw clasp. Come back through a few beads.
5. On the other end, string an 11º, a crimp tube, an 11º, the dangle from step 1, and the ring. Come back through a few beads. Check the fit and adjust, if needed. Crimp the crimp tubes and trim the excess wire.

 **tip**

While neither symmetrical nor asymmetrical, this bracelet showcases each bead without casting one as a focal, and it offers another way of letting the materials tell the story. Is your eye drawn to the polymer clay disks, the wavy gemstone, or the stacks of shells? It really doesn't matter. Since a bracelet will turn as you wear it, I knew this design would work from any angle.

DESIGN SKILL

Brights

These bright beauties are the star of the show. Use black or white "pacers" as a neutral backdrop for a stunning look. Bright beads need balance, so remember what you've learned about pacing a design. The pacer beads will fade to the background and allow the brights to take center stage. They also work to offset the beads so each stands out— important when you're using multiple colors. Don't be afraid to go big as well as bright. You might as well make a statement!

Bright bracelet

1. Cut the flexible beading wire 5–6 in. (13–15cm) longer than your desired bracelet length.
2. String an alternating pattern of rondelles and 4mm round beads.
3. Check the fit, and add or remove 4mms if necessary.
4. String a crimp tube, a 4mm, and half the clasp. Come back through the beads just strung and tighten the wire. Crimp the crimp tube and trim the excess beading wire.
5. Repeat on the other end.

Materials

Finished length: 7½ in. (19.1cm)

12 8x12mm faceted rondelles in **3** colors

17 4mm round beads, black

2 crimp tubes

Toggle clasp

Flexible beading wire

tip This black clasp blends into the background of this design, yet it is big enough to support the large beads. A silver clasp would have pulled the focus of the bracelet away from the bright beads.

Turquoise and black necklace

Materials

Finished length: 17½ in. (44.5cm)

7 12mm round beads

78-88 4mm round beads

2 crimp tubes

2 crimp covers (optional)

Lobster claw clasp and closed ring

Flexible beading wire

1. Cut a piece of beading wire 6 in. (15cm) longer than your desired necklace length.

2. String a 12mm and three 4mms. Repeat with the remaining 12mms, ending with a 12mm.

3. On each end, string an equal number of 4mm beads until the necklace is your desired length (allow about an inch for the clasp).

4. On one end, string a crimp bead and the clasp. Go back through a few beads at the end of the necklace. Crimp the crimp tube. Repeat on the other end, substituting the ring for the clasp. Trim the excess wire.

5. Attach crimp covers over the crimps.

White and blue necklace

Materials

Finished length: 16½ in. (41.9cm)

3 12mm round acrylic beads

3 10mm round acrylic beads

3 8mm round acrylic beads

66 8° seed beads (more for a longer necklace)

2 crimp tubes

5mm soldered jump ring

Lobster claw clasp

Flexible beading wire

1. Cut a piece of flexible beading wire to your desired length plus about 6 in. (15cm).

2. Center a 12mm acrylic bead on the wire. On each end, string a seed bead and a 12mm.

3. On each end, string an alternating pattern of 10mms and seed beads.

4. On each end, string an alternating pattern of 8mms and seed beads.

5. String seed beads on each end until you've reached the desired length.

6. String a crimpt tube, a seed bead, and the clasp. Come back through the beads and crimp the crimp tube. Repeat on the other end with the soldered jump ring.

tip

Flip the perspective in this design, and use the bright beads as the backdrop and the neutrals as the focal.

Black and white bracelet

Materials

Finished length: 7½ in. (19.1cm)

12mm round acrylic bead

2 10mm round acrylic beads

12 8mm round acrylic beads, **4** white and **8** black

2 8º seed beads

4 3mm round beads

2 crimp tubes

Clasp

Flexible beading wire

1. Cut a piece of flexible beading wire to your desired length, plus a few inches.

2. Center a seed bead, the 12mm, and a seed bead on the wire.

3. On each end, string a black 8mm, a white 8mm and a black 8mm.

4. On each end, string a white 10mm.

5. Repeat step 3.

6. On each end, string a 3mm, a crimp tube, a 3mm, and half the clasp. Come back through a few beads.

7. Check the fit. Crimp the crimp tubes and trim the excess wire.

The turquoise seed beads add just the pop of color this bracelet needs and leave no doubt that the 12mm is the focus of the bracelet.

DESIGN SKILL

Neutrals

Understated elegance or casual class, neutrals are a wardrobe staple. These projects are a perfect example of letting the materials dictate the design. In a neutral palette, texture plays an important role. Choose materials that are visually interesting. Neutral beads also provide an opportunity for experimentation with non-traditional metals for the findings and finishings. Copper and brass have warmth and richness but no sparkle or flash. These softer tones are ideal for completing a neutral ensemble.

Brown and copper necklace

Nut-like round beads are featured here. Wood ovals, round textured lava rock beads, and a copper clasp complete the story.

1. Cut a piece of flexible beading wire 6 in. (15cm) longer than your desired finished length. Center a 15mm round on the wire.

2. On each end, string a 6mm round, a 10mm oval, two 6mms, a 10mm oval, a 6mm, and a 15mm. Repeat once.

3. On each end, string a repeating pattern of 6mms and 10mm ovals until the necklace is about 2 in. (5cm) shorter than the desired length.

4. On each end, string two crimp tubes, a 6mm, and a clasp half. Come back through a few beads. Check the fit and adjust, if necessary. Crimp the crimp tubes and trim the excess wire.

Materials

Finished length: 20 in. (51cm)

5 15mm round beads (nut, wood, or seed)

16 10mm oval wood beads

36 6mm round lava rock beads

2–4 crimp tubes

Toggle clasp

Flexible beading wire

tip

Copper crimp tubes match the clasp, but sometimes they are not as strong as sterling silver. Since this necklace is long and a little heavy, I used two crimp tubes on each end.

Gemstone and brass necklace

Materials

Finished length: 25 in. (64cm)

13 15mm round gemstone beads

28 8mm brass trade beads

74 8mm lentil gemstone beads

4 8° seed beads

2 crimp tubes

Clasp and ring

Flexible beading wire

These lovely large round chalcedony beads are accented with brass trade beads and lentil gemstones.

1. Cut a piece of flexible beading wire 6 in. (15cm) longer than your desired finished length. Center a 15mm round on the wire.
2. On each end, string a lentil, a 8mm brass bead, three lentils, a brass bead, a lentil, and a 15mm. Repeat until the necklace is close to the desired length.
3. Finish the necklace with a pattern of lentils and brass beads (the 15mms are not comfortable at the back of your neck).
4. On each end, string a crimp tube, two 8° seed beads, and a clasp half. Come back through a few beads. Check the fit and adjust, if necessary. Crimp the crimp tubes and trim the excess wire.

tip **Using an odd number of 15mm beads means one will be centered on your necklace and the pattern will be balanced on each side.**

DESIGN SKILL

Changing Findings, Beads, and Clasps

When you design your own jewelry, you need to give careful thought to each element of the piece, from the focal bead, to the accent beads, to the finishing touches such as the earring wires or clasps. The point of this section is for you to see (literally) how small changes can affect the mood or the vibe of a piece of jewelry. For example, in some projects I've made the exact same designs using very different beads, and in other projects, I've used the same beads but changed the earring wires or the clasps. I hope you can see the difference and apply what you learn to your own decision making as you shop for materials for your projects.

Clasp swap

Findings are not an afterthought. They are a critical part of your design. When it comes to clasps for necklaces and bracelets, there are a few things to keep in mind:

DO choose a clasp that completes the tone—whether bold, whimsical, or dainty—of your design.

DO choose a sturdy clasp for heavy beads.

DO keep scale in mind. A pattern with larger beads **(A)** can handle a more substantial finish, while a diminutive design **(B)** needs a subdued clasp.

DO use a large clasp if you are short on beads or using expensive materials—it can extend your length by almost an inch **(D)**.

DO match a color in the beads. One bracelet is all about the brass accents **(C)**, while another emphasizes the black glass beads **(E)**. Same pattern, same beads, different mood.

findings swap

Earring wires and other findings can have a great impact on jewelry design. Think of the mood you want to set. Understated or traditional? Choose standard earring wires that will blend in, leaving the focus on the dangle. More modern? Choose the marquis or the hoop and balance the earring wire design with a simple dangle. The French hoop gives a jaunty look and calls for a fringe of drops.

Three pairs of earrings with flower dangles include post, hoop, and oversized kidney shaped.

Three pairs of earrings with pinch beads show marquis, standard fish hook, and French hoops. The style of the earring wire establishes the mood of the earring.

Bead swap

In these examples, the pattern is the same, but the beads and findings are very different. You can see how color alone influences the mood of the piece. Keep this in mind as you make projects from this book. Follow the step-by-step directions to make the jewelry, but choose materials that are right for you.

The earrings are from p. 24. See the difference in a monochromatic black and silver approach when compared to the bright green and blue? Bead sizes and shapes are similar, and the findings are exactly the same.

Key to my heart necklace

The only difference in these two necklaces is that the black necklace uses sets of beads for the chain embellishments, making the links the same size as the oval crackle beads in the red necklace.

1. Make the dangles: String an 8mm crystal on a headpin and make a wrapped loop above the bead; string a 4–6mm bicone, an oval, and a 4–6mm on a headpin and make a wrapped loop above the bead.

2. Use a 5mm jump ring to attach each dangle and the charm to the 8mm jump ring or decorative ring.

3. Cut the chain into a 7-in. (18cm) and a 23-in. (58cm) piece.

4. Find the center of the 7-in. piece, and connect the decorative ring or 8mm jump ring.

5. Make two connector links: Trim the head from a headpin. On one end, make the first half of a wrapped loop. String an oval bead, and make the second half of a wrapped loop.

6. Link one end of a connector to an end of the 7-in. chain, and complete the wraps. Repeat with the other end of the connector and an end of the 23-in. chain.

7. Repeat step 6 with the remaining connector and the remaining chain ends.

Materials

Finished length: 32 in. (81cm)

25mm key charm

3 18mm oval beads

6 4–6mm bicone crystals

6–8mm bicone crystal

8mm jump ring or decorative ring

4 5mm jump rings

2 headpins

32 in. (81cm) chain

Techniques
Review

Open and close a plain loop or jump ring

1. To open a formed loop, grasp it with two pairs of pliers, held parallel to each other.

2. Gently push the loop open by moving one set of pliers forward and the other set backward.

3. Repeat the process in reverse to close the loop. Resist trying to "unroll" the loop—this will overwork and weaken the wire, and you'll never get a perfectly round loop the second time.

Make a plain loop

1. To make a plain loop above a bead, trim the end of the wire to 3/8 in. (1cm), and bend it at a right angle against the bead. To make a plain loop at the end of a wire, grasp the wire with chainnose pliers 3/8 in. from the end and make a right-angle bend.

2. Grasp the tip of the wire with roundnose pliers and feel to be sure that the wire is flush with the edge of the pliers. If you feel a stub of wire, you've grasped too far away from the tip, so adjust your pliers. Gently roll the wire until you can't roll comfortably anymore.

3. Gently roll the wire until you can't roll comfortably.

4. Reposition the pliers, and continue to roll the loop. The tip of the wire should meet the corner of your initial bend, and you should have a perfect, centered wire circle.

Make a wrapped loop

1. To make a wrapped loop above a bead, trim the wire about 1 ¼ in. (3.2cm) above the bead.

2. Grasp the wire with chainnose pliers above the bead. Fold the wire over the pliers into a right-angle bend. If you're working with plain wire (no bead), grasp the wire about 1 ¼ in. down from the end and make a right-angle bend over the pliers.

3. Switch to roundnose pliers, and position the jaws in the bend. Bring the end of the wire up and over the top jaw of the pliers, and as far down as you can.

4. Reposition the roundnose pliers so the lower jaw is in the loop. Slide the wire down the shaft to be sure that you are working in the same place as you did in step 2. Curve the wire downward around the bottom of the pliers, until the tail is at a right angle to the stem. This is called "the first half of a wrapped loop." At this stage, you can add dangles to the loop or connect the loop to another element, such as a link of chain.

5. To finish the wrapped loop, switch back to chainnose pliers. Position the pliers' jaw across the loop, as shown.

6. Use a second pair of pliers—roundnose or chainnose—to grasp the wire at the end and begin to wrap this piece around the exposed stem. One wrap will secure the loop, but several wraps look nicer. Be sure to fill in the entire gap between the loop and the bead so the bead is secure.

Wrap above a top-drilled bead

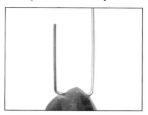

1. Cut a 3-in. (7cm) length of wire, and center a top-drilled bead on the wire. Bend each side upward to form a squared-off U shape. Leave a tiny bit of room for the bead to move (about 1mm).

2. Cross the wires into an X shape above the bead.

3. Use chainnose pliers to bend one wire straight up and one wire to the side. They'll form a right angle at their intersection.

4. Wrap the horizontal wire around the vertical wire as in a wrapped loop. Make two or three wraps and trim the wire.

Flatten a crimp

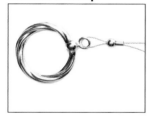

1. String a crimp tube, a spacer bead, and half of the clasp on a wire. Bring the wire end back through the spacer bead and the crimp tube.

2. Hold the crimp tube using the tip of chainnose pliers. Squeeze the pliers firmly to flatten the crimp. Tug the clasp to be sure the crimp has a solid grip.

Make a folded crimp

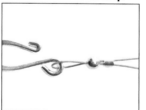

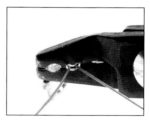

1. Position the crimp tube in the notch closest to the pliers' handle.

2. Separate the wires, and firmly squeeze the crimp.

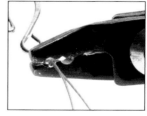

3. Move the crimp to the notch at the pliers' tip, and squeeze the crimp tube, folding it in half at the indentation made in step 2.

4. Tug to be sure the crimp is secure.

Overhand knot

Make a loop and pass the working ends through it. Pull the ends to tighten the knot.

Surgeon's knot

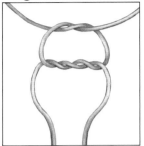

1. Cross the right end over the left end and go under and over the cord. Go over and under again.

2. Cross the left end over the right end and go through once. Pull the ends to tighten the knot.

3. Optional: Glue the knot with a flexible glue such as G-S Hypo Cement.

Lark's head knot

1. Fold a cord in half and lay it behind a ring, loop, etc. with the fold pointing down.

2. Bring the ends through the ring from back to front, then through the fold and tighten.

Acknowledgments

My daughters, Haley and Meredith, are a constant source of inspiration and delight. I do what I do for you.

I am well supported by a wide circle of friends and family and I thank each and every one for encouraging me.

Special thanks to the artists that I am fortunate to work with every day. Your work inspires me.

And finally, thank you to my colleagues at Kalmbach Publishing, Dianne, Mary, Erica, Lisa, Jim, and Bill, for sharing my vision and helping to bring this project to life.

About the author

Karin has been making things all her life, but jewelry design became her passion in 2003 when she was associate editor during the inaugural year of *Bead Style* magazine. Many, many necklaces, bracelets, and earrings later, Karin still remembers the challenges of being new to a hobby, and brings the beginner's perspective to any class she teaches.

Her design philosophy is centered on perfecting basic skills to make simple, elegant, and wearable jewelry. This focus is reflected in her books, including *The Absolute Beginners Guide: Stringing Beaded Jewelry* and *Mostly Metals: A Beginner's Guide to Jewelry Design*. When she's not making jewelry, writing about it, teaching others, or taking a class herself, Karin enjoys other hobbies including sewing, gardening, and cooking.

Karin currently works for Kalmbach Books as a senior editor. She lives in Oconomowoc, Wis. with her two daughters.

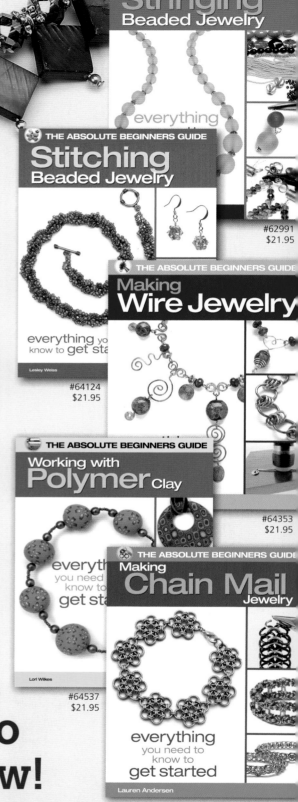